BLACK AMERICANS OF DISTINCTION

IMPORTANT BLACK AMERICANS IN
Business and Commerce

Kristina Castillo

San Diego, CA

About the Author

Kristina Castillo is a writer originally from South Carolina. She writes books for children and teens.

© 2023 ReferencePoint Press, Inc.
Printed in the United States

For more information, contact:
ReferencePoint Press, Inc.
PO Box 27779
San Diego, CA 92198
www.ReferencePointPress.com

ALL RIGHTS RESERVED.
No part of this work covered by the copyright hereon may be reproduced or used in any form or by any means—graphic, electronic, or mechanical, including photocopying, recording, taping, web distribution, or information storage retrieval systems—without the written permission of the publisher.

LIBRARY OF CONGRESS CATALOGING-IN-PUBLICATION DATA

Names: Castillo, Kristina C., author.
Title: Important Black Americans in business and commerce / by Kristina Castillo.
Description: San Diego, CA : ReferencePoint Press, Inc., 2022. | Series: Black Americans of distinction | Includes bibliographical references and index.
Identifiers: LCCN 2021059094 (print) | LCCN 2021059095 (ebook) | ISBN 9781678202842 (library binding) | ISBN 9781678202859 (ebook)
Subjects: LCSH: African American businesspeople--Biography--Juvenile literature. | Successful people--United States--Biography--Juvenile literature. | African American business enterprises--Juvenile literature.
Classification: LCC HC102.5.A2 C38 2022 (print) | LCC HC102.5.A2 (ebook) | DDC 338.090089/6073 [B]--dc23/eng/20220228
LC record available at https://lccn.loc.gov/2021059094
LC ebook record available at https://lccn.loc.gov/2021059095

CONTENTS

Introduction   4
Black Americans in Business

Chapter One   8
Madam C.J. Walker: Creator of a Beauty Empire

Chapter Two   17
Ottawa W. Gurley: Founder of Black Wall Street

Chapter Three   27
Oprah Winfrey: Media Mogul

Chapter Four   37
Ursula Burns: CEO of a Fortune 500 Company

Chapter Five   46
Sean Combs: Hip-Hop Mogul and Entrepreneur

Source Notes   55
For Further Research   59
Index   61
Picture Credits   64

INTRODUCTION

Black Americans in Business

In 2021 only 7 of the 724 billionaires in the United States were Black. The same year only four Black chief executive officers (CEOs) led Fortune 500 companies, the five hundred largest US corporations in terms of sales revenue as ranked by *Fortune* magazine. Although Black Americans make up approximately 14 percent of the US population, Black Americans own only 2 percent of US businesses, according to 2018 data from the US Census Bureau. Despite these statistics, there are countless stories of successful Black entrepreneurs and business leaders who have transformed American lives.

History of Black Entrepreneurship

Although the Thirteenth, Fourteenth, and Fifteenth Amendments to the Constitution were intended to secure freedom for Black Americans after the Civil War, many suffered under various states' Jim Crow laws that continued discrimination and segregation. Segregation denied Black people access to services available to White people and ensured that Black people were separated from White people in all aspects of life. However, segregation allowed Blacks to start their own businesses in Black communities in the late 1800s and early 1900s. Thus, "segregation patterns . . . created market opportunities for black entrepreneurs to step in, make money and meet the demands of the black community,"[1] explains Mehrsa Baradaran, author of *The Color of Money: Black Banks and the Racial Wealth Gap*. Black businesses were born to serve Black customers, from barbershops and restaurants to hotels and nightclubs. Some Black Americans acquired great wealth during this time, such as Mary Ellen Pleasant and Robert Reed Church, who were a couple of the first Black Americans to become millionaires.

Throughout history, the business achievements of Black Americans have typically trailed those of White Americans. For example, it took eighty-five years after White oil titan John D. Rockefeller became the first American billionaire for Robert F. Smith to become the first Black American billionaire in 2001. As of 2021 Smith is still the wealthiest Black American, with an estimated fortune of $6 billion, which he earned through his private equity fund.

Recently, the COVID-19 pandemic has accelerated the creation of new Black-owned businesses. Michelle Youngblood, a Black woman from Illinois, was laid off during the pandemic and decided to pursue something she had always loved—design. She used her final paycheck to start a children's clothing company, which sells its goods online. Others have also started businesses because they too lost their jobs during the pandemic.

Ongoing Obstacles for Black-Owned Businesses

A major obstacle for Black-owned businesses is the lack of access to money (capital), which is a legacy of racism and discrimination. According to Bloomberg News, as of 2021 the average White household in the United States has approximately seven times more wealth than the average Black household. This racial wealth gap was created by slavery, segregation, and other racial inequalities. Obtaining loans from banks is also difficult for Black-owned businesses for similar reasons. Black-owned businesses are 20 percent less likely than White-owned businesses to obtain

Former American Express CEO Kenneth Chenault (pictured) was one of the first Black Americans to run a Fortune 500 company. Chenault has described the lack of diversity in corporate America as embarrassing.

a loan from a large bank, according to a 2021 article by management consulting firm McKinsey & Company.

In the wake of the Black Lives Matter protests in 2020, some large banks and corporations pledged efforts to support Black-owned businesses. Several Black business leaders have started funds to support Black entrepreneurs and minority-owned businesses. For example, Black real estate tycoon R. Donahue Peebles announced a $500 million fund for minority and women real estate developers. Although providing capital is not the only way to support Black businesses, Keenan Beasley, the chair and executive director of nonprofit Venture Noire, says it is a vital step. "Through the creation of more [Black-owned] businesses, we're creating more jobs and creating more income for a group that is historically underfunded and underutilized," he explains. "We still have a long way to go, but fueling the growth of minority-owned businesses is the right way to establish an equitable entrepreneurial ecosystem—and a thriving U.S. economy."[2]

The Slow Climb to the Top

In addition to becoming entrepreneurs, some Black Americans have successfully climbed the corporate ladder to assume top positions with large companies. As CEO of American Express from 2001 to 2018, Kenneth Chenault was one of the first Black Americans to run a Fortune 500 company. However, despite some advances in increasing diversity in the upper ranks of companies, Black people are still largely absent from the governing boards and top positions of most large companies. Chenault described the lack of diversity in corporate America as embarrassing: "It's embarrassing because there are thousands of black people who are just as qualified or more qualified than I am who deserve the opportunity, but haven't been given the opportunity."[3]

> "We still have a long way to go, but fueling the growth of minority-owned businesses is the right way to establish an equitable entrepreneurial ecosystem—and a thriving U.S. economy."[2]
>
> —Keenan Beasley, chair and executive director of Venture Noire

Despite obstacles, Black Americans have demonstrated resilience and creativity in the business world. The business successes and contributions of historical and contemporary Black Americans are inspiring a new generation of entrepreneurs and business leaders. And with expanding educational opportunities and paths toward white-collar jobs, more Black Americans are finding more lucrative positions within America's growing economy.

CHAPTER ONE

Madam C.J. Walker: Creator of a Beauty Empire

In 2020 Netflix released a series about a Black woman who created a beauty empire: *Self-Made: Inspired by the Life of Madam C.J. Walker*. Although the series has been criticized for certain factual inaccuracies, it sparked a resurgence in interest in how Madam C.J. Walker quickly built a successful business of hair and beauty products designed for Black women, which she sold across the United States and internationally.

Orphaned at a young age and forced to work as a child, Walker wanted something different for her life, something better than the life she was born into. Perhaps even more, she wanted a better life for her daughter, including a formal education, which Walker lacked. With $1.25, relentless determination, and a smart business mind, Walker started her company in her kitchen. According to the *Guinness Book of World Records*, Walker was the first self-made female millionaire. However, her legacy extends beyond her wealth. As Walker improved her own life, she sought to bring other Black women along with her and donated to causes to elevate the lives of all Blacks. She inspired her daughter and countless other daughters to dream big and to turn problems into opportunities.

Picking Cotton and Washing Clothes

On December 23, 1867, Sarah Breedlove, later known as Madam C.J. Walker, was born to two former slaves in Delta, Louisiana. Unlike her older four siblings, who were born into slavery, she was born free.

Walker's parents were sharecroppers. However, both of her parents had died by the time she was seven, and she moved in with her older sister and brother-in-law. The three later moved to Vicksburg, Mississippi, where Walker worked in the cotton fields with her sister and likely worked as a domestic servant as well. Her only formal education was three months of literacy classes at a church as a child and occasional public night school as an adult.

When she was fourteen years old, she married Moses McWilliams. Many historians claim that she married McWilliams to escape the abuse of her brother-in-law. Walker and McWilliams had one daughter, Lelia, when Walker was seventeen. However, two years later, McWilliams died when Walker was twenty. In 1889 Walker—a widow and single mother of a three-year-old daughter—headed north to St. Louis, Missouri, where her brothers lived and worked as barbers. This provided her first glimpse into the world of professional hair care.

For income, Walker worked as a laundress, which only earned her about $1.50 a day, but the job allowed her to watch her daughter while washing and ironing clothes at home. Although she had little money, she was determined to provide a good life for her daughter. "As I bent over the washboard and looked at my arms buried in soapsuds, I said to myself: 'What are you going to do when you grow old and your back gets stiff? Who is going to take care of your little girl?'"[4] Walker said to the *New York Times* in 1917.

> "As I bent over the washboard and looked at my arms buried in soapsuds, I said to myself: 'What are you going to do when you grow old and your back gets stiff? Who is going to take care of your little girl?'"[4]
>
> —Madam C.J. Walker

Turning a Hair Problem into Opportunity

Walker had no formal education, washed clothes for a living, and was self-conscious about her hair—which was brittle and falling out. "During the early 1900s, when most Americans lacked indoor plumbing and electricity, bathing was a luxury," explained Walker's great-great-granddaughter, A'Lelia Bundles, who has written prolifically about Walker. "As a result, Sarah and many other women were going bald because they washed their hair so infrequently, leaving it vulnerable to environmental hazards such as pollution, bacteria and lice."[5]

According to Bundles's biography of Walker, *Self-Made*, Walker started experimenting with store-bought and homemade formulas to heal her scalp issues. Around the same time, she met Annie Malone, who sold a product called the Great Wonderful Hair Grower. Malone, a Black woman originally from Illinois, had a successful hair care business that she relocated to St. Louis, where Walker was living. Walker enrolled in Malone's cosmetics school and began selling Malone's hair products around 1904.

In St. Louis, Walker started dating Charles Joseph Walker, a salesperson. They moved to Denver, Colorado, in 1905, where she continued selling Malone's products. She married Charles Walker in 1906 and called herself Madam C.J. Walker, in reference to the French cosmetics industry, where "Madam" (sometimes spelled "Madame") was used to imply distinction and authority. Walker had bigger dreams; instead of selling someone else's products, she wanted to develop and sell her own line of hair care products for Black women. At the time, when Jim Crow laws segregated Black and White people, starting a business for Black customers was one of the few ways out of poverty. There were even fewer opportunities for Black women than Black men. However, Walker saw an opportunity with hair care products; after all, she had been selling Malone's products and understood the market.

Walker created her own products, which she started selling in 1906. According to Walker, her formula for her top-selling product,

Competitor Annie Malone

Many accounts of Walker's life reference a rivalry between Walker and Annie Malone. In many respects, the women were similar. Like Walker, Malone was born to former slaves, orphaned at a young age, and raised by a sibling. Both developed hair products for Black people and sold them door-to-door before employing sales agents to sell the products around the United States. Both built beauty empires, became wealthy, and donated money to a variety of causes. A'Lelia Bundles, Walker's great-great-granddaughter and biographer, says, "There's no doubt in my mind that Madam C. J. Walker and Annie Malone both are important historical figures who made major contributions as early twentieth century hair care industry pioneers and philanthropists."

According to Bundles, neither woman invented the system for cleaning and healing the scalp. Bundles explains that the basic recipe for the remedy used by both women appeared in medical texts as early as the 1700s.

Malone outlived Walker, and her company's success peaked in the 1920s. However, after a series of legal matters, including divorce, Malone's wealth declined before her death in 1957.

A'Lelia Bundles, "The Facts About Madam C. J. Walker and Annie Malone," *A'Lelia Bundles Blog*, 2020. https://aleliabundles.com.

Madam C.J. Walker's Wonderful Hair Grower, came to her in a dream: "A big Black man appeared to me and told me what to mix up for my hair. Some of the remedy was grown in Africa, but I sent for it, mixed it, put it on my scalp, and in a few weeks my hair was coming in faster than it had ever fallen out. I tried it on my friends; it helped them. I made up my mind I would begin to sell it."[6] In addition to the secret recipe hair grower, Walker's early products included Glossine (a pressing oil) and a vegetable shampoo.

Walker started selling her products door-to-door. She expanded by selling at church meetings and community gatherings and

With $1.25, relentless determination, and a smart business mind, Madam C.J. Walker built a successful business of hair and beauty products designed for Black women. She is said to be America's first self-made female millionaire.

eventually through a mail-order catalog. Her husband became her business partner and assisted with marketing and promotion. She advertised in Black newspapers throughout the country to expand her geographic reach. After traveling for over a year with her husband promoting her products, she settled in Pittsburgh, Pennsylvania, and opened a beauty school. There, she taught other Black women how to care for and style hair. She encouraged women to follow the Walker System, which included using hot combs that straightened hair. Many people criticized Walker for encouraging Black women to emulate White beauty standards by straightening their hair. However, Walker claimed that her system was not designed specifically to straighten hair; instead, her formula and the tools used in hair care were intended to heal the scalp.

Building an Empire

In 1910 Walker and her family left Pittsburgh and moved to Indianapolis, Indiana, where she incorporated her business as the Madam C.J. Walker Manufacturing Company. In Indianapolis she built a factory, hair salon, beauty school, and laboratory to support her research. She later expanded by building beauty schools across the United States. While her business was thriving, her marriage to Charles Walker was ending, punctuated by divorce in 1912.

Consistent with her goal to empower Black women, she trained Black women to be sales agents, known as Walker Agents, allowing them to earn commissions. "At a time when unskilled white workers earned about $11 a week, Walker's agents were making $5 to $15 a day, pioneering a system of multilevel marketing that Walker and her associates perfected for the black market,"[7] historian Henry Louis Gates Jr. says. At the height of her career—from 1911 to 1919—she employed as many as twenty thousand women as Walker Agents. In addition, she taught women how to budget, start their own businesses, and become financially independent. According to Nancy Davis, curator emeritus at the Smithsonian National Museum of American History in Washington, DC, Walker "created educational opportunities for thousands of black women and provided them jobs and careers, and opportunity to make money, and to make money in their own community."[8]

Despite her successful business, Walker was not always supported by her peers. At the time, most influential Black business leaders were men. In 1912 Walker requested an opportunity to speak at the National Negro Business League convention, which was held in Chicago. The league's founder, Booker T. Washington, refused her request.

> "[Walker] created educational opportunities for thousands of black women and provided them jobs and careers, and opportunity to make money, and to make money in their own community."[8]
>
> —Nancy Davis, curator emeritus at the Smithsonian National Museum of American History

Nevertheless, Walker attended, and toward the end of the convention, she stood up and spoke to a mostly male audience:

> Surely you are not going to shut the door in my face. . . . I have been trying to get before you business people to tell you what I am doing. I am a woman who came from the cotton fields of the South. I was promoted from there to the washtub. Then I was promoted to the cook kitchen. And from there I promoted myself into the business of manufacturing hair goods and preparations.[9]

After commanding the league's attention, she no longer had to request time to address the audience. Instead, she was an invited speaker at the convention the following year.

Her assertiveness and ambition only grew. She saw opportunities beyond the borders of the United States and expanded internationally. In 1913 she began selling her products in parts of Central America and the Caribbean. After a two-month trip to these regions, she successfully recruited sales agents in countries such as Haiti, Costa Rica, Panama, Cuba, and Jamaica.

Spending Her Fortune

In 1916 Walker moved to Harlem, New York, where her now-adult daughter had moved previously. She opened the Walker Salon at 108 West 136th Street, which served as the Harlem headquarters for her business. After her move, she became more involved in politics and joined the executive committee of the New York chapter of the National Association for the Advancement of Colored People (NAACP). In 1917 she and other business leaders from Harlem visited the White House to try to convince President Woodrow Wilson to make lynching a federal crime. However, Wilson refused to meet with them. Despite the disappointment, Walker continued to work on antilynching campaigns. She also donated $5,000 to the NAACP's antilynching fund, which was the largest gift from an individual that the NAACP had ever received at the time.

Mentor Alice Kelly

Walker lacked a formal education, but she did not let that hold her back from succeeding in business. Instead, she surrounded herself with well-educated people and sought to educate herself as an adult. In that respect, she hired Alice Kelly, a former teacher at the African American Eckstein Norton Institute in Cane Spring, Kentucky, as her personal tutor. Kelly later became the manager and foreperson of Walker's factory in Indianapolis, Indiana. Kelly was one of the few people who knew the formulas for Walker's products.

Kelly also served as Walker's traveling companion. Violet Davis Reynolds, who was a secretary at the Walker company, explained that Walker turned to Kelly for assistance with her presentations: "Whenever I traveled with them, I remember Madam asking Miss Kelly immediately after her speech, 'How did I do? How can I do better?'"

After Walker relocated to New York, Kelly continued managing the Walker factory. Kelly served on several community organizations in Indianapolis and donated money to help fund a new building for a local branch of the YWCA that served Black women.

Quoted in A'Lelia Bundles, "Madam Walker's Mentors, Sister Friends & Rivals," *A'Lelia Bundles Blog*, 2020. https://aleliabundles.com.

While embracing activism, she was still devoted to growing her business and empowering her sales agents. In 1917 she organized the Madam C.J. Walker Hair Culturists Union of America and the National Negro Cosmetics Manufacturers Association. The same year, she held the first Madam C.J. Walker Hair Culturists Union of America convention, which was one of the first gatherings of female American entrepreneurs. The convention allowed the women to network and share their success stories as Walker Agents.

With an increasing amount of wealth, Walker hired a Black architect to design her estate in Irvington, a wealthy White suburb in Westchester County, New York. One of her neighbors was John D. Rockefeller, America's first billionaire, who made his fortune from oil. Her estate, known as Villa Lewaro, was intended to become a gathering spot for Black Americans.

However, Walker did not have much time to enjoy her estate. In 1919, one year after her estate was completed, she died from kidney disease at age fifty-one. She was reported to be the wealthiest Black woman in the United States at the time of her death, with an estimated net worth of $500,000 to $1 million. Her wealth was self-made, which she earned from her beauty empire in just thirteen years. According to Walker's obituary in the *New York Times*, "She said herself two years ago [in 1917] that she was not yet a millionaire, but hoped to be some time, not that she wanted the money for herself, but for the good she could do with it."[10] In her will, she gifted almost $100,000 to orphanages, educational institutions, and individuals and directed two-thirds of her estate's future net profits to charity.

Inspiring Social Entrepreneurship

After her death, her daughter, Lelia (then known as A'Lelia), continued running the company until she died in 1931. Then A'Lelia's adopted daughter took control. The company ultimately closed in 1981. Walker's Hair Culturists Union of America conventions continued through the 1960s. Her business model of using Walker Agents and multilevel selling provided road maps for other cosmetics companies like Avon and Mary Kay.

Walker's success story not only reverberated in her lifetime by lifting other women out of poverty but also inspired entrepreneurs for generations that followed. "Today we talk a lot about social entrepreneurship and businesses having a double bottom line or triple bottom line, [maximizing social and environmental good as well as profits]," Tyrone Freeman, a professor at Indiana University and author of *Madam C. J. Walker's Gospel of Giving*, explains. "I see Walker doing this 100 years ago."[11]

Walker once said that she was not handed a "royal flower-strewn path to success. . . . Whatever success I have attained has been the result of much hard work and many sleepless nights. I got my start by giving myself a start. So don't sit down and wait for the opportunities to come. You have to get up and make them for yourselves!"[12]

CHAPTER TWO

Ottawa W. Gurley: Founder of Black Wall Street

On June 1, 2021, President Joe Biden marked the one hundredth anniversary of the Tulsa Race Massacre, during which a vibrant Black community known as Black Wall Street was destroyed by an angry mob of White Oklahomans. As acknowledged by Biden, the massacre was largely ignored by history and not taught in most classrooms until recently:

> For much too long, the history of what took place here was told in silence, cloaked in darkness. But just because history is silent, it doesn't mean that it did not take place. And while darkness can hide much, it erases nothing. It erases nothing. Some injustices are so heinous, so horrific, so grievous they can't be buried, no matter how hard people try. . . .
>
> As soon as it happened, there was a clear effort to erase it from our memory—our collective memories—from the news and everyday conversations. For a long time, schools in Tulsa didn't even teach it, let alone schools elsewhere.[13]

One of the men responsible for building Black Wall Street was Ottawa W. Gurley. As his story is shared, it is inspiring a new generation of Black entrepreneurs who share similar visions of economically prosperous communities of color.

Growing Up in Arkansas

On December 25, 1868, Ottawa (spelled Ottowa in some sources) W. Gurley was born in Huntsville, Alabama, to former slaves. Soon after his birth, Gurley's parents moved to Pine Bluff, Arkansas, where he grew up as one of at least six children. Although little has been written about his childhood, some accounts claim that Gurley was largely self-educated, whereas others claim Gurley obtained a degree in education from the Branch Normal College, which is now the University of Arkansas at Pine Bluff.

Gurley worked a variety of jobs in his early career, including teacher and US Postal Service employee. Gurley ultimately resigned from the US Postal Service and married his childhood sweetheart, Emma Evans.

Sensing New Opportunities

When Gurley sensed a new opportunity, he and his wife left Arkansas and headed west to Oklahoma to participate in the Cherokee Outlet Land Rush in Indian Territory. The federal government had obtained land in the northern part of Oklahoma from the Cherokee tribe, and the land rush was an opportunity for settlers to claim a parcel. On September 16, 1893, twenty-five-year-old Gurley lined up with one hundred thousand other people to race at a given signal and claim acreage. After traveling 50 miles (80 km), he placed a flag in the ground, claiming land in Perry, Oklahoma, about 80 miles (129 km) east of Tulsa. There he served a short stint as a school principal and then opened a general store with his wife.

A little over a decade later, Gurley pursued a different line of work in Tulsa after oil was discovered in the area. As news spread that Tulsa had oil, over one hundred oil companies opened nearby, and those companies needed people to work the oil fields. Gurley sold his general store in Perry and moved with his wife to Tulsa, anticipating that more Black people in search of opportu-

J.B. Stradford

J.B. Stradford, another founder of Black Wall Street, was born in Kentucky. The son of a freed slave, Stradford attended college in Ohio and then returned to Kentucky, where he worked as a school principal. There he witnessed a heinous act: the lynching of a Black man. No longer feeling safe in Kentucky, Stradford moved to Indiana, where he opened a bicycle shop and a barbershop and earned his law degree in 1899.

In 1905 he moved to Tulsa. Like Gurley, he was drawn to Tulsa's economy and purchased property in the Greenwood District. "By the beginning of 1917," Stradford wrote in an unpublished memoir, "I had amassed quite a fortune. I owned 15 rental houses, a sixteen-room brick apartment building. . . . I decided to realize my fondest hope . . . and that was to erect a large hotel in Tulsa, exclusively for my people." In 1918 the Stradford Hotel had its grand opening. Like everything else on Black Wall Street, Stradford's businesses were destroyed during the massacre. Soon after, he was arrested and charged with inciting the riot. Amid threats of being lynched, Stradford fled Tulsa and never returned.

Quoted in Tucker C. Toole, "Thousands Lost Everything in the Tulsa Race Massacre—Including My Family," *National Geographic*, May 28, 2021. www.nationalgeographic.com.

nity would move there too. In 1905 Gurley bought 40 acres (16.2 ha) of land in North Tulsa and divided the property into residential and commercial lots to realize his vision: to build a community for Black people created by Black people. The following year Gurley opened a new general store and a rooming house on a dirt road that later became Greenwood Avenue, which was named after Greenwood, Mississippi, from which many of the area's earliest inhabitants had moved.

Gurley was right that Tulsa would experience an influx of Black residents. Black people moved to Tulsa in packed wagons to escape increasing lynching and racial violence in the South and for a chance at a better life. Although Tulsa was more progressive than the South, it was not free from racism. For example, Oklahoma law prohibited Black people from working the good-paying jobs in the oil fields. However, there were plenty of other jobs, such as domestic work, as well as opportunities to open businesses in Tulsa. As a result of the area's economic prosperity, Tulsa was dubbed the Magic City, and its population grew rapidly between 1910 and 1920. The total population quadrupled to more than seventy-two thousand, while the Black population grew from less than two thousand to almost nine thousand. And a large Black community sprang up around Greenwood Avenue.

Building Black Wall Street

Gurley partnered with another Black entrepreneur, John the Baptist (J.B.) Stradford, to create a vibrant and prosperous Black community. Together, Walker and Stradford invested in businesses, leased commercial space, rented apartments, and loaned money to other entrepreneurs. Soon the Greenwood area was named Negro Wall Street by educator and prominent Black leader Booker T. Washington because of the large number of Black-owned businesses located there. Because Jim Crow laws essentially enforced racial segregation, Greenwood "was an economy born of necessity," Hannibal B. Johnson, author of *Black Wall Street*, explains. "It wouldn't have existed had it not been for Jim Crow segregation and the inability of Black folks to participate to a substantial degree in the larger white-dominated economy."[14]

> "[Black Wall Street] wouldn't have existed had it not been for Jim Crow segregation and the inability of Black folks to participate to a substantial degree in the larger white-dominated economy."[14]
>
> —Hannibal B. Johnson, author of *Black Wall Street*

By 1920 Gurley was a real estate broker in Greenwood. The Greenwood community spanned over thirty-two city blocks and was nearly self-sufficient with Black-owned businesses—from doctors' offices and restaurants to saloons and funeral homes. Many of the community's businesses were owned or financed by Gurley.

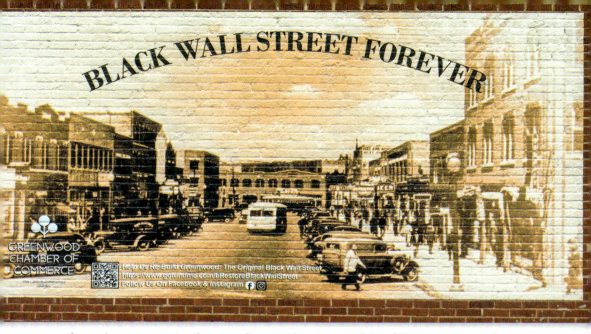

A mural commemorates the once vibrant and prosperous Tulsa, Oklahoma, community known as Black Wall Street. Real estate developer and entrepreneur Ottawa W. Gurley helped build this community, which was destroyed by an angry White mob in 1921.

Greenwood had two newspapers, a YMCA, and a post office substation. There were multiple churches—including the Vernon AME Church cofounded by Gurley—a hospital, a roller-skating rink, and schools in the Greenwood District. Two luxury hotels were in the district: the Gurley Hotel, owned by Gurley, and the Stradford Hotel, owned by Stradford. Every dollar spent in Greenwood was estimated to circulate in the Black economy nearly thirty times. "You had the wealthy, middle class, the poor Blacks all living on the same block, and so many of those individuals who started out in the working class, because they lived there, would eventually go on to own their own business in the Greenwood district," Michael Carter Sr., founder and national president of the Black Wall Street USA national movement, says. "That's a result of Gurley's contributions."[15]

> "You had the wealthy, middle class, the poor Blacks all living on the same block, and so many of those individuals who started out in the working class, because they lived there, would eventually go on to own their own business in the Greenwood district."[15]
>
> —Michael Carter Sr., founder and national president of Black Wall Street USA

The Women of Black Wall Street

The story of Black Wall Street is largely told through a male perspective: about the Black men who founded Black Wall Street and the White men who burned it down. However, one of the earliest written accounts of the Tulsa Race Massacre was written by a Black woman named Mary E. Jones Parrish. Parrish, who operated a typing school in Black Wall Street, published her book, *Events of the Tulsa Disaster*, in 1922 to tell her own story as well as other survivors' accounts.

In addition to Parrish, there were other women who owned or operated businesses in the Greenwood District. For example, Susie Bell owned and ran two restaurants where Black professionals and church leaders often met. Even Gurley's wife, Emma, purchased property in the area in her name and ran the Gurley Hotel.

Women of Black Wall Street (WBWS), along with its website, was created to profile these pioneering women, including Parrish, Bell, and Gurley. According to the website, WBWS "captures the experiences of Black Greenwood women to add to the larger story of this dynamic community."

Women of Black Wall Street, "About the Project," 2021. https://blackwallstreetwomen.com.

Education was highly valued in Greenwood, and teachers were among the highest-paid workers. An elite high school named after Booker T. Washington exposed students to Latin, algebra, physics, music, and art—a curriculum that prepared students for prestigious colleges.

Growing Racial Tension

Despite Greenwood's success, it was largely ignored by the White politicians, and the poorer blocks in Greenwood lacked many basic services, such as paved roads and proper sewage lines. Further, as the concentration of Black people grew in Greenwood, many White people in Tulsa grew concerned about the district, its visible poverty, and its supposed vices. Racism was fueled by local newspaper articles and White preachers, as well as politicians throughout Oklahoma.

Because Gurley had a good relationship with important White people in Tulsa, he was appointed sheriff's deputy by the city of Tulsa, charged with policing the Black community. Some residents of Greenwood criticized him for his relationships with White people and his approach to dealing with racism. Unlike Stradford, who adopted a more confrontational approach to racism, Gurley was deemed too conciliatory by some residents. He often brokered deals with the White sheriff to avoid conflict between law enforcement and Black men who argued for equal treatment under the law. However, when Gurley sought justice for a Black woman who had accused a White man of assaulting her on a train, things changed. Although Gurley successfully obtained a warrant for the man's arrest, the sheriff prohibited Gurley from serving the warrant, explaining that he would not allow a Black man to serve a warrant on a White man in Tulsa. When Gurley realized he had less power than he believed, he turned his badge in, resigning as a sheriff's deputy around 1919.

Firing of a Gun

Racial tensions in Tulsa exploded on May 30, 1921, when a Black man was arrested for allegedly sexually assaulting a White woman on an elevator. Because the exact details of what happened next have been described differently by historians, the Oklahoma legislature appointed a commission to investigate the event in 1996. It is generally agreed that hundreds of White people gathered at the Tulsa courthouse, demanding that the sheriff release the Black man so that they could lynch him, but the sheriff refused. When word spread to the Greenwood District, residents held discussions to decide the proper response. According to legal scholar Alfred L. Brophy, Gurley tried to convince a crowd gathered outside of his hotel that the deputy sheriff had assured him there would be no lynching, but the crowd did not believe him.

Thereafter, a group of Black men, including World War I veterans carrying guns, headed to the courthouse to stop the lynching. Their arrival seemed to attract more White people, drawing a crowd as large as two thousand people, many with guns. Hours later, a second group of Black men arrived at the courthouse, offering their services to the sheriff to protect the man from being lynched. Soon after their arrival, there was an argument between a White man and a Black man that resulted in the firing of a gun, which initiated what is known as the Tulsa Race Massacre. Gunfire rang out from both sides, killing approximately a dozen men in front of the courthouse. Because the Black men were outnumbered, they retreated to the Greenwood District.

Burning It Down

According to the Oklahoma commission, officials deputized White men to commit violent acts and provided some with firearms, ammunition, and badges. In the early morning of June 1, 1921, a White mob entered the Greenwood District, killing people on the streets and in their homes. Then the mob started burning down Black Wall Street. "I'll never forget the violence of the white mob," Viola Fletcher, a 107-year-old survivor of the massacre, recounted to Congress in 2021. "I still see Black men being shot, Black bodies lying in the street. I still smell smoke. . . . I still see Black businesses being burned. . . . I live through the massacre every day."[16] According to testimony provided by Gurley in an insurance case arising from the massacre, Gurley was ordered out of his hotel before it was burned:

> Those were white men, they was wearing khaki suits, all of them, and they saw me standing there and they said, "You better get out of that hotel because we are going to burn all of this . . . stuff, better get all your guests out." And they rattled on the lower doors of the pool hall and the restaurant, and the people began on the lower floor to get out, and I told the people in the hotel, I said "I guess you bet-

ter get out." There was a deal of shooting going on from the elevator or the mill, somebody was over there with a machine gun and shooting down Greenwood Avenue, and the people got on the stairway going down to the street and they stampeded.[17]

There are accounts of planes dropping explosives, which flattened buildings. The government offered no real assistance to stop the killings or the destruction of property. By the time the massacre ended that evening or early the next morning, June 2, as many as three hundred people had been killed. Most of the victims were Black, and the dead were buried in unmarked mass graves, some of which have still not been located. Black Wall Street burned to the ground in what has been described as "the single worst incident of racial violence in American history"[18] by Scott Ellsworth, a historian and author of *Death in a Promised Land: The Tulsa Race Riot of 1921*.

Although Gurley and his wife survived the massacre, it stole the majority of his fortune. Although accounts differ, the Oklahoma commission states that Gurley was worth $157,783—approximately $2.3 million in 2021—before his businesses burned. Black people who survived the massacre were arrested by units of the Oklahoma National Guard and placed in internment camps for weeks or even months. Gurley and his wife were no exception.

> "Those were white men, they was wearing khaki suits, all of them, and they saw me standing there and they said, 'You better get out of that hotel because we are going to burn all of this . . . stuff, better get all your guests out.'"[17]
>
> —Ottawa W. Gurley

After Gurley and his wife were released from an internment camp, they moved to Los Angeles, California, where they ran a small hotel. Gurley died fourteen years later at age sixty-seven. Ultimately, no one was ever convicted for the heinous crimes committed during the massacre.

Laying the Groundwork for Economically Strong Black Communities

Despite losing his fortune, Gurley has inspired others to open businesses and fight for economic opportunity for the Black community. According to Black Wall Street USA founder Carter, Gurley "laid the groundwork for our generation to pick it up and run with it." He adds, "What Gurley did was for the long term—for the generations who never would have met him."[19]

Gurley was not the only person to lose wealth in the massacre. Practically all of the area's business owners and residents lost their businesses and homes. According to John W. Rogers Jr., chair of Ariel Investments and great-grandson of J.B. Stradford, Black Wall Street's businesses were worth an estimated $50 million in today's dollars. However, none of that money was able to be reinvested, and the wealth was never able to accrue to Black families. "The effects of us not having multi-generational wealth and not having economic opportunity continues in our society today," Rogers says. "Unfortunately so many times in our history, when Black folks get a few steps ahead, we get pulled back down. . . . It's why the wealth gap in this country is so dramatically worse than it was 25 or 40 years ago."[20]

CHAPTER THREE

Oprah Winfrey: Media Mogul

Airing in November 2021, Oprah Winfrey's interview of Adele allowed the music superstar to open up about her personal life as well as the inspiration for her latest album. Winfrey's intimate talks have encouraged many of her interviewees to discuss their unique experiences as both private and public figures. Adele is among a long list of celebrities and world leaders interviewed by Winfrey throughout her career as a talk-show host and media personality.

Perhaps celebrities are so candid with Winfrey because she has often spoken openly about her own journey through balancing fame with personal well-being. Winfrey had to break racial and gender barriers and overcame a series of traumas on her rise to become one of the most influential people in the world. In addition to hosting *The Oprah Winfrey Show* for twenty-five years, she has acted, produced television shows and films, created a television network, and published a magazine. As the first Black female billionaire, she has built a career out of being a storyteller, which starts with being a good listener.

Surviving a Difficult Childhood

Winfrey's rise was a triumph that she could not have predicted at a young age. She was born on January 29, 1954, into poverty in rural Mississippi to a teenage single mother. She was named Orpah after the biblical character in the book of Ruth, but people always mispronounced her name as Oprah, which she continues to use. Her grandmother, Hattie Mae Lee, initially raised Winfrey. Lee introduced Winfrey to the church, where she regularly recited scripture aloud, earning her the nickname of "Preacher."

When Winfrey was six years old, Lee became sick, and Winfrey moved to inner-city Milwaukee, Wisconsin, to live with her mother, with whom she had a complicated relationship. Winfrey was the victim of repeated sexual abuse: she was first raped by an older cousin when she was nine and later raped by other family members during her teenage years.

Excelling in School

Despite her abusive home life, Winfrey excelled in school, where she was supported by caring teachers. She says, "A teacher saved my life, Mrs. Duncan in the fourth grade . . . she was the first person I thought really saw me."[21] She credits her teachers for inspiring her original career aspiration: teaching. "For so many years in my life that's the only place I ever really felt loved. And it's the reason why for so many years I wanted to be a teacher, to be able to give to other kids what my teachers had given to me."[22] She never became a teacher, but her teachers' influence was long lasting.

During her teenage years, Winfrey had other mentors. Eugene Abrams, a university professor who was helping out at her school, recognized Winfrey's intellect and helped her gain admission to one of the best high schools in Milwaukee. "You were the most curious 13-year-old I ever ran across," Abrams told Winfrey. "You always had a book and you always had a question."[23]

Winfrey did not stay in Milwaukee much longer and could not reap all the benefits of the elite high school. In 1968, when Winfrey was fourteen, she became pregnant. Winfrey's mother sent her to live with her father in Nashville, Tennessee. Her baby was born prematurely and died in the hospital soon after birth. She kept her pregnancy a secret and returned to school as if nothing happened. "I went back to school and told no one," she says. "My fear was that if I were found out, I would be expelled."[24]

Past Traumas

Throughout the years, Oprah Winfrey has opened up about her traumas, including whippings by her grandmother and the sexual abuse she suffered as a child. Instead of hiding her pain, she has allowed audiences and readers insight into how these events have impacted her life.

Some of her recent ventures have highlighted her traumas. For example, Winfrey and psychiatrist Bruce D. Perry recently released the book *What Happened to You? Conversations on Trauma, Resilience, and Healing*. In the book's introduction, Winfrey recalls, "The long-term impact of being whipped—then forced to hush and even smile about it—turned me into a world-class people pleaser for most of my life." She says it took "half a lifetime to learn to set boundaries and say 'no' with confidence." Nevertheless, she credits her childhood with helping her develop a strong sense of independence.

She also recently teamed up with England's Prince Harry for a documentary series on Apple TV+ called *The Me You Can't See*. In the series, both Winfrey and Harry open up about their traumas alongside other celebrities and noncelebrities in a series of conversations aimed at shining a light on mental health.

Bruce D. Perry and Oprah Winfrey, *What Happened to You? Conversations on Trauma, Resilience, and Healing*. New York: Flatiron, 2021.

In high school in Nashville, Winfrey was engaged in a variety of activities, such as student government, debate, and drama club. Her first job as a teenager was working at a grocery store next to her father's barbershop. By the time she was sixteen, she had landed a job at a local radio station reading the news on the air; this was the first of many jobs that paid her to talk.

By the time she graduated high school, she had earned a full scholarship to Tennessee State University, a historically Black institution in Nashville, studying communications. She was one credit short of graduating when she left college in 1976 to coanchor the news at the WJZ-TV station in Baltimore. Eventually, in

Oprah Winfrey, renowned for her interviews with celebrities and world leaders, has created a media empire that has earned her the distinction of being the first Black female billionaire. To reach this point, she has overcome personal trauma as well as racial and gender barriers.

1986 she turned in her final paper and earned her college degree, which her father had encouraged her to complete.

Breaking In

At age nineteen, while still attending college in Tennessee, Winfrey coanchored the news at Nashville's WTVF-TV; she was both the youngest news anchor and the first Black female news anchor at the station. In 1976, when she moved to Baltimore at age twenty-two for a new job at a television station, she began as a coanchor on the six o'clock news. However, months after she started, she was fired from the coanchor position and demoted to lower-profile positions at the station. Winfrey was embarrassed by the demotion, especially given that the station had heavily advertised her arrival as the new coanchor, including a promo called "What is an Oprah?" As she was shuffled through a variety of other jobs at the station, she recalls being treated differently from her male colleagues. At one point, one of her male supervisors demanded that his girlfriend live in Winfrey's apartment for free, and Winfrey felt like she had no choice but to accept.

However, after the demotion, another opportunity arose. She was asked to cohost, with Richard Sher, WJZ-TV's local talk show called *People Are Talking*. After taping the first show in 1978, she knew that her days as a news reporter were over and her new career as a talk-show host had begun. "There was no doubt that the seeds of what was to give my life meaning and purpose had been planted," Winfrey writes in her book *The Path Made Clear: Discovering Your Life's Direction and Purpose*. "That day, my 'job' ended and my calling began."[25] During her time at WJZ-TV, she also met one of her best friends, Gayle King. Winfrey says of King, who is currently a cohost for the television show *CBS Mornings*, "She is the mother I never had; she is the sister everybody would want; she is the friend everybody deserves."[26]

Taking the Spotlight

At age thirty, Winfrey moved to Chicago in 1984 to host WLS-TV's low-rated thirty-minute morning talk show, *AM Chicago*. Within months, the show became the highest-rated talk show in Chicago. Given her success in turning the show around, the show was renamed *The Oprah Winfrey Show*, and the first episode aired nationwide on September 8, 1986. In the beginning *The Oprah Winfrey Show* was considered a tabloid talk show. However, by the mid-1990s Winfrey adapted her show to cover a broad array of topics, such as health, spirituality, and politics. She interviewed celebrities about social issues with which they were concerned, started Oprah's Book Club, and hosted televised giveaways, including giving everyone in her audience a new car in one episode. She shared personal stories about herself, including painful ones such as her history of sexual abuse.

Her hour-long show launched many careers by featuring guests, highlighting her favorite products, or discussing books. When Winfrey shared a product she loved with her audience, they listened. "Oprah has made a commitment to her guests over the years that anything she found in her life, that she considered to really be of value, whether it was a certain kind of hair dryer or a book or a professional or whatever, she would share with her audience,"[27] says Phil McGraw, whose own career catapulted based on her endorsement, including his self-help show entitled *Dr. Phil*. Her influence is so profound that it has been dubbed "the Oprah effect."

Her talk show was the highest-rated daytime talk show in US television history and the recipient of over forty-seven Daytime Emmy Awards. Winfrey wanted to end her show on a high, before it fizzled out. Given changes in the media world and in consumers' behaviors, including the desire to watch programs on demand instead of live, Winfrey decided that the time was right to conclude a monumental chapter in her career. After twenty-five years, the final episode of *The Oprah Winfrey Show* aired on May 25, 2011.

According to Winfrey, she interviewed over thirty-seven thousand people on *The Oprah Winfrey Show*. Her secret to good interviewing is listening. "There's not a human being alive who doesn't want—in any conversation, encounter, experience with another human being—to feel like they matter," she says. "And you can resolve any issue if you could just get to what it is that they want—they want to be heard. And they want to know that what they said to you meant something."[28] Her fourth-grade teacher, Mary Duncan, was on *The Oprah Winfrey Show* and reminded Winfrey that she was a good listener at an early age:

> "Oprah has made a commitment to her guests over the years that anything she found in her life, that she considered to really be of value, whether it was a certain kind of hair dryer or a book or a professional or whatever, she would share with her audience."[27]
>
> —Phil McGraw, television talk-show host

"You were quiet, and furthermore, if anyone else was talking you would put your finger to your lips and remind them that you should be listening."[29]

Expanding into Other Media

In addition to her talk show, Winfrey has been involved in a variety of other media ventures. She cofounded Oxygen, a women's cable television network. She also founded Harpo Productions, a film and television production company that has produced shows like *The Oprah Winfrey Show*, *Dr. Phil*, *Rachael Ray*, and *The Dr. Oz Show* and films such as *Selma*, *When They See Us*, and *Beloved*. She created a popular monthly magazine, *O, The Oprah Magazine*, which was published for over twenty years. In the digital space, she started Oprah.com, which is a women's lifestyle website that offers advice on health, food, home, and relationships, as well as provides resources related to her other media.

Each venture provides a new set of challenges for Winfrey, and some have even been considered failures, at least temporarily. For example, in 2011 OWN: Oprah Winfrey Network was launched as a new television channel with Discovery Communications. However, the network did not take off as expected; her talk-show audience did not flock to the network, and OWN struggled with ratings. "I was stressed and I was frustrated and quite frankly I was actually embarrassed,"[30] Winfrey said in a 2013 commencement address at Harvard University, when discussing OWN's early years. Winfrey did not give up on OWN, and it has since become a successful network. More recently, she has joined forces with Apple to create new original programs exclusively for Apple's streaming

> "There's not a human being alive who doesn't want—in any conversation, encounter, experience with another human being—to feel like they matter. And you can resolve any issue if you could just get to what it is that they want—they want to be heard. And they want to know that what they said to you meant something."[28]
>
> —Oprah Winfrey

service, Apple TV+. Oprah has produced several shows for Apple TV+, including *Oprah's Book Club*, *Oprah Talks COVID-19*, and *The Oprah Conversation*.

As her career indicates, Winfrey is not afraid to fail, because she views failure as a chance to learn new information and an opportunity to move toward something better. She is also not afraid to pivot into new media or explore new opportunities if something is not working or circumstances are changing. She says that she is always guided by her internal voice, which assures her that everything will be okay.

Supporting Education

Winfrey is one of the wealthiest women in the United States. In 2021 she had a fortune totaling $2.6 billion, according to *Forbes*. Throughout her career, she has been a philanthropist, donating money to a variety of causes, particularly those that support education. She believes that one of the greatest ways to empower and change an individual's life is through education. Much of her philanthropy has evidenced that belief. For example, through Oprah's private charity—the Oprah Winfrey Charitable Foundation—she has awarded hundreds of grants to organizations that educate and empower women, children, and families around the world. She also established the Oprah Winfrey Leadership Academy Foundation and has contributed more than $40 million to create a boarding school for girls in grades seven through twelve in South Africa, which opened in 2007. She inspired the creation of the public charity Oprah's Angel Network, which was established in 1998 and raised more than $80 million to support various causes, including women's shelters and youth centers.

More recently, she was the largest donor to the National Museum of African American History and Culture, which opened in 2016, giving $21 million to ensure that the museum would open. In 2019 she donated $13 million to Morehouse College, an all-male historically Black college, in Atlanta, Georgia. In 2020 Win-

Mentor Maya Angelou

Maya Angelou, who is most recognized as a poet and memoirist, profoundly impacted Oprah Winfrey's life. They first met when Winfrey interviewed Angelou as a reporter in Baltimore in the 1970s. They reconnected in Chicago in 1984, after which Angelou was often featured on *The Oprah Winfrey Show* and in *O, The Oprah Magazine*.

However, Winfrey felt a connection to Angelou before even meeting her. Upon reading Angelou's autobiography *I Know Why the Caged Bird Sings*, Winfrey recognized their childhood similarities, including a southern upbringing and being the victim of rape. "Meeting Maya on those pages was like meeting myself in full. For the first time, as a young black girl, my experience was validated."

Their connection grew throughout their lives until Angelou died in 2014. After her death, Winfrey recounted Angelou's many lessons, which ranged from how to embrace aging to how to forgive. "Her greatest lesson to me: 'You are enough!'"

Oprah Winfrey, "Oprah Talks to Maya Angelou," *O, The Oprah Magazine*, December 2000. www.oprah.com.

Oprah Winfrey, "What Oprah Knows for Sure About Her Teacher and Friend Maya Angelou," Oprah.com. www.oprah.com.

---

frey established a $12 million COVID-19 Relief Fund to support organizations in cities that she has called home throughout her life. She encourages other wealthy individuals to look in their own communities to discover ways to serve.

Inspiring Others to Share and Listen

Winfrey has paved the way for other Black women in the media. Wendy Williams, host of the talk show *The Wendy Williams Show*, acknowledged Winfrey's influence on her career. "I certainly couldn't be where I am today, hosting my own daytime talk show, if she hadn't come before me, so I'd just like to thank her

> "I certainly couldn't be where I am today, hosting my own daytime talk show, if [Winfrey] hadn't come before me, so I'd just like to thank her for that."[31]
>
> —Wendy Williams, host of *The Wendy Williams Show*

for that,"[31] says Williams. Shonda Rhimes, a television producer and screenwriter who created hit shows such as *Grey's Anatomy* and *Scandal*, grew up watching *The Oprah Winfrey Show* and credits Winfrey's success for showing her what was possible for a Black woman in television.

Winfrey's greatest legacy may be inspiring people to tell their stories, especially the difficult ones. Throughout her career, she has shared her professional and personal challenges, hoping that she could inspire others to break free from the shame of carrying secrets, such as being the victim of sexual abuse. Recently, she has expressed interest in helping bridge the deep divide between people in the United States, which she attempted to do by hosting roundtable discussions of voters after the 2016 presidential election and asking them to do what she has been doing her whole career: listen.

CHAPTER FOUR

Ursula Burns: CEO of a Fortune 500 Company

Ursula Burns's memoir, *Where You Are Is Not Who You Are*, was released in 2021. It describes her path to becoming CEO of Xerox in 2009 and how she felt as the first Black woman to obtain the top position of a Fortune 500 company. By the time she became the company's CEO, she had spent almost thirty years at Xerox climbing the corporate ladder as a loyal and hardworking employee. Burns credits her mother for inspiring her to dream big and to leave every place better than she found it. Although she has since moved on from her role at Xerox, she continues to lead companies and promote diversity in the high ranks of corporate America.

Setting High Expectations

Ursula Burns was born on September 20, 1958, to parents who immigrated to the United States from Panama. She was raised by her mother, alongside her two siblings, in a low-income housing project on the Lower East Side of New York City. When she was growing up, the project where she lived was known for gang violence and drug activity. Burns's mother was very influential in her life, ensuring that she received a good education and avoided the trouble lurking in her neighborhood. To provide for the family, her mother worked a wide array of jobs,

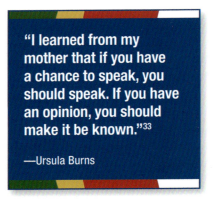

"I learned from my mother that if you have a chance to speak, you should speak. If you have an opinion, you should make it be known."[33]

—Ursula Burns

including running a child-care center out of their apartment. To ensure they had health care, her mother cleaned a doctor's office in the neighborhood.

"Many people told me I had three strikes against me: I was black. I was a girl. And I was poor,"[32] Burns says. She never saw it that way. Neither did her mother, who set high expectations for her, often telling her that where she grew up did not define her. In addition, she credits her mother for her strong work ethic and teaching her to speak her mind. "I learned from my mother that if you have a chance to speak, you should speak. If you have an opinion, you should make it be known,"[33] Burns said in the PBS documentary *Makers: Women Who Make America*.

Despite limited means, Burns's mother paid for her to attend Cathedral High School, an all-girls Catholic school, where she excelled, particularly in math. When she was in school, a guidance counselor told her she had three career options—teacher, nun, or nurse—none of which appealed to her. Instead, she wanted to be an engineer. She earned a scholarship to the Polytechnic Institute of New York University in Brooklyn, New York, where most of her classmates were White men. Although she questioned whether she belonged, she focused on her studies and eventually discovered her love for mechanical engineering.

When she graduated from college, there were no expectations that she, as a Black woman, could ever lead a global company. "I can assure you that no one at my commencement was pointing at me and predicting that I would become a CEO," Burns said during her 2009 commencement address at Rochester Institute of Technology. "Women presidents of large global companies were non-existent. Black women presidents of large companies were unimaginable."[34] After college, Burns earned a master's degree in mechanical engineering from Columbia University, paid for by Xerox, where she would work for most of her career.

Mentorship

In her memoir, Ursula Burns highlights the importance of mentors, beginning with her first mentor, her mother. At Xerox Burns had several other mentors, including Anne Mulcahy, who preceded her as CEO. Another important mentor was Vernon Jordan, who started out as a civil rights lawyer before moving into the corporate world, including a stint as a Xerox director. Later he became an adviser to President Bill Clinton and President Barack Obama.

Early in Burns's career, Jordan introduced himself to her in the hallway at Xerox and followed up with a list of recommended reading. After that, he offered years of advice and guidance, which helped her climb the ranks to CEO. Burns describes Jordan as a guide throughout her life. "Literally, every important moment in my life, my daughter's birth, important moments in my career, my husband's illness, my husband's eventual death, my promotions, appointment to boards, every single thing in my life from the time that I met him was—Vernon was there, every important moment," she recalls. After he died in 2021, Burns said, "I try my best to kind of emulate him, because he is the perfect example of a friend."

Quoted in *PBS NewsHour*, "Vernon Jordan, Civil Rights Leader and Presidential Confidant, Dies at 85," March 2, 2021. www.pbs.org.

Seizing Opportunities

Although she did not know it at the time, her very first career decision was critical. In 1980 she obtained a summer internship at Xerox, which was the premier company in document technology, primarily manufacturing copiers and printers. Her office was located in Rochester, New York, which was the manufacturing headquarters for Xerox at the time. "I didn't think, when I walked into the company, that I would be the CEO," she recalls. But she did expect to excel: "I *did* expect to be successful, though. My mother raised us to think that if we worked hard, and if we put our end of the bargain in, it would work out OK for us."[35]

Former Xerox CEO Ursula Burns was the first Black woman to obtain the top position of a Fortune 500 company. She continues to lead companies and promote diversity in the high ranks of corporate America.

Over the next decade, Burns held various positions in product development and planning operations at Xerox. Climbing the corporate ladder was not easy for a Black female engineer with no formal business education, but she climbed it. She found that the more she advanced in engineering, the more she learned business, which increased her interest in that side of the company. For example, one of her earliest business tasks was pricing a machine she was developing with a team at Xerox, which required her to focus on the value the customer would place on the machine and therefore devise a price such customers would pay for it.

In 1990 Wayland Hicks, a senior executive at Xerox, asked Burns to be his assistant. Initially, she was hesitant to accept the position because she thought it was secretarial or administrative work. Nevertheless, she seized the opportunity, which turned out to be a career milestone. As Hicks's assistant, she interacted with Xerox's executives and earned their respect. She also sat in on meetings with corporate executives and was not afraid to speak her mind. For example, she noticed that Xerox's leadership consistently expressed an intention to cut back on hiring but never followed through, always hiring more employees. During a meeting with Xerox's then-chair and chief executive Paul Allaire, Burns raised her hand and said, "I'm a little confused, Mr. Allaire. If you keep saying, 'No hiring,' and we hire 1,000 people every month, who can say 'No hiring' and make it actually happen?"[36] Allaire did not answer her question and continued with the meeting. Later, Allaire asked to see Burns in his office, and Burns was convinced it was bad news. Contrary to her expectations, she was offered a job working for him.

As a result, she became executive assistant to Allaire in 1991. In that role—a role for which she originally felt she was overqualified—she traveled with Allaire and saw firsthand how to run a global enterprise. Allaire encouraged her to continue to speak up and to empower other employees to feel a sense of ownership in the company.

Climbing the Ladder

In 1999 she was named the company's vice president of global manufacturing, overseeing a team tasked with making network printers. However, in 2000 Burns decided to leave Xerox, given that the company was not succeeding as it previously had been. The company asked her to stay, and it was the first time she understood how much Xerox valued her. It was also the first time she thought there was a possibility she could become CEO one day if she continued with Xerox. Once again, she followed her mother's advice to "leave the place—any place you are—a little bit better than you came in"[37] and continued working at Xerox, which had room for improvement.

> "The thing I valued most about Ursula, and why I valued her participation in senior management, is that she has the courage to tell you the truth in ugly times."[38]
>
> —Anne Mulcahy, former CEO of Xerox

By 2000 she was promoted to senior vice president. In 2001 Anne Mulcahy became CEO of Xerox, which was historic: Mulcahy was the first female CEO of a Fortune 500 company. Mulcahy was impressed by Burns's skills and mentored her. She notes, "The thing I valued most about Ursula, and why I valued her participation in senior management, is that she has the courage to tell you the truth in ugly times."[38] Mulcahy, like Burns, was a longtime employee of Xerox, and Burns and Mulcahy worked well together. As a mentor, Mulcahy supported Burns and helped pave the way for Burns to take over the company.

Becoming a First

After working at Xerox for almost thirty years, Burns became CEO of the company in 2009 and was the first Black female CEO of a Fortune 500 company. Burns made headlines and received accolades, given the historical significance of her promotion. Although she initially enjoyed the attention, she grew tired of it because she had not yet accomplished anything in her new role. There was a lot she needed to do to transform Xerox. At the time, Xerox, which was a pioneer in printing and photocopying, was losing its brand prestige in a world that was dominated by digital technologies. Instead of basking in the media attention, she got to work, following another piece of her mother's advice praising the value of hard work.

Under Burns's leadership, Xerox moved from a hardware company that manufactured copiers and printers to a software-oriented company, allowing the company to remain relevant and competitive in the digital world. She recognized that customers needed help managing their documents through archival and retrieval services. Burns, who is known for being fearless, was not afraid to try new ideas in these areas, which helped expand the company's offerings and ensured that Xerox maintained strong earnings during her tenure.

Working Abroad

When Burns was thirty-six, her boss asked her to relocate to London to run Xerox's European operation. In her memoir, she recalls packing up her husband and two young children and moving to London for three years. They lived in a large, American-style house near walking trails and playgrounds, and they enjoyed exploring their new surroundings. "We did all the British stuff we could and had a wonderful time."

Her management position required her to run a large team stationed across the world. Her position in London was challenging, particularly managing people who were older than her, but she learned a lot from the experience. "From a business perspective, I had a huge amount of independence—setting plans to be in Spain one day, the northern part of London the next—and I really enjoyed that." Being away from Xerox's home office helped her mature and gain confidence. She considers her assignment in London to be a vital stepping stone to becoming CEO.

Ursula M. Burns, *Where You Are Is Not Who You Are*. New York: Amistad, 2021.

Being CEO required that she have a security guard drive her to her meetings and accompany her on Xerox's private plane. However, she drove herself to and from the office whenever possible, and when she was being driven around, she preferred sitting in the passenger seat instead of in the back. She never felt like she belonged to the CEO club, because her life experiences had been quite different from other CEOs. Unlike the CEOs of other companies, she did not have a summer home in popular vacation spots for the wealthy. She also believed another factor that separated her from other CEOs was her disinterest in golf. She did not golf and thought it was a waste of time, taking many hours out of the day. She preferred spending free time with her family and friends, most of whom were not in the corporate world. Of course, the most obvious differences between her and other CEOs were her race and gender.

In 2016, after she completed the job she intended at Xerox, she left the company after thirty-six years of service. She did not have a retirement party or receive lavish gifts—per her request—and took only a few objects from her office, leaving behind awards and books she had collected over the years. One of the objects she kept was a photo of her family with President Barack Obama at the White House when she was appointed vice chair of the President's Export Council. "That was huge for me," she says. "Here was the first African American president of the United States honoring me, the first African American woman CEO of a Fortune 500 company."[39]

Giving Back

While still at Xerox, Burns was appointed by Obama to help lead the White House science, technology, engineering, and mathematics (STEM) program, which was tasked with promoting STEM education. Burns believes that STEM education is key to addressing pressing global problems, which will gain urgency in the future. "We have to feed seven to 10 billion people. We have to get them water that's potable and clean. We have to be able to move them around in some kind of reasonably efficient way. . . . There is not one thing that I mentioned . . . that you can solve without a good STEM team around it."[40]

Since retiring from Xerox in December 2016, Burns has continued to work and serve. She has held positions at several companies, including the telecom giant VEON and Teneo, a public relations firm. Burns has served as a board director for a variety of companies, including Uber, where she has worked to expand the popular ride-sharing business to other countries. She also provides leadership counsel to nonprofits and educational institutions, such as the Massachusetts Institute of Technology.

In 2020 she donated $1 million to the HistoryMakers, a video oral history archive responsible for collecting the stories of extraordinary Black Americans. Before her donation, the archive had fewer stories of Black women than Black men. Her donation helped launch the WomanMakers Initiative, allowing

180 interviews of leading Black American women to be added to the archive.

Increasing Diversity

Despite her success as a CEO, few Black women have achieved her rank in other companies; as of 2021 only two of the CEOs of Fortune 500 companies were Black women. Burns hopes to inspire more racial and gender diversity in the upper ranks of companies, including boardrooms. In that respect, she leads the Board Diversity Action Alliance, which takes steps to increase the representation of racially and ethnically diverse directors on corporate boards. Burns believes that diversity is not optional for companies hoping to remain relevant in today's world, which is more diverse than ever.

Burns's success is inspiring to others. Lisa DeFrank-Cole, director of leadership studies at West Virginia University says:

> Marian Wright Edelman once said, "You can't be what you can't see," and I think this quote is appropriate when describing the impact of Ursula Burns. As the first black woman to serve as CEO of a major corporation, she has not only made history, but has given hope and inspiration to many girls who may want to follow her path. She has become a role model for women, and especially women of colour, around the world.[41]

Burns's mother did not live long enough to see her daughter's success. Her mother died when Burns was only twenty-five years old and still a relatively new employee at Xerox. However, today as a veteran executive in business affairs, she is still following her mother's advice and trying to make her proud.

> "As the first black woman to serve as CEO of a major corporation, [Burns] has not only made history, but has given hope and inspiration to many girls who may want to follow her path. She has become a role model for women, and especially women of colour, around the world."[41]
>
> —Lisa DeFrank-Cole, director of leadership studies at West Virginia University

CHAPTER FIVE

Sean Combs: Hip-Hop Mogul and Entrepreneur

In the summer of 2021, Sean Combs announced on social media that he would be releasing a new album later in the year, twenty-four years after his debut album, *No Way Out*. Combs is well known for his hip-hop music and fashion line. However, his business ventures are vast. As he has evolved from a young college student working at Uptown Records to an entrepreneur with a diverse portfolio, his public persona has evolved too. Throughout his life, he has gone by different names, from Puffy to Love. To him, the name changes signify shifts in his life, a way of reinventing himself. Despite facing a number of personal losses, he has persevered and succeeded in business. Given recent announcements of new endeavors, including the launch of a rhythm and blues (R&B) record label, he has no intention of stopping anytime soon.

Hustling from a Young Age

Sean Combs was born on November 4, 1969, in the Harlem area of New York City. After his father was murdered when Combs was three years old, he was raised by his mother in Harlem until they moved to Mount Vernon, New York, when Combs was twelve. His Harlem roots have informed his identity. Combs says about growing up in Harlem:

You're empowered by knowing your history. You can envision Malcolm X speaking on 125th, the '20s at the Cotton Club, Langston Hughes, Harry Belafonte, Lorraine Hansberry. . . . There was such a deep sense of culture. When you're born in Harlem, you're taught how to dress nice on $5. You understand presentation, where your sneakers always have to be fresh, and the necessity of dance. . . . We're just natural-born hustlers.[42]

He attended a Catholic school in the Bronx, where according to a 1998 interview with *Jet*, he was called Puffy because he had a temper when he was a kid. Over the years, he would be called many other names: Puff Daddy, P. Diddy, Diddy, and most recently, Brother Love or simply Love.

From an early age, Combs had an entrepreneurial spirit. He credits his mother, who often worked four or five jobs, for inspiring his interest in accomplishing things through hard work. When he was twelve years old, Combs obtained his first job delivering newspapers. "At the time, I wasn't old enough to work legally, so I made a deal with the paper boys who were leaving for college. I told them to let me deliver their papers and I'd send them half of the money. By the time I was 13, I had six routes."[43] Simply having the job was not enough for Combs; he wanted to excel. Given that most of his customers were elderly, he took extra care with his deliveries, ensuring that the newspapers were placed inside the screen door for easy retrieval. He believed that providing a high level of customer service was important, and he has carried that belief to all of his business endeavors. As a teen, he also worked as a busboy at a Mexican restaurant and operated a lemonade stand.

After graduating high school, he attended Howard University in Washington, DC, where he studied business. However, he never completed his studies, because he got involved in the music industry. Nevertheless, Howard University awarded him an honorary doctorate in 2014.

Storming the Music Industry

While attending Howard University, Combs obtained an internship at Uptown Records in New York City and commuted between there and Washington, DC, until he left college. He excelled at Uptown Records and was quickly promoted to vice president of talent and marketing. In that role, he helped launch the careers of Mary J. Blige and Jodeci. Although he had no training in music production, he had a natural talent for identifying songs that would be hits. Despite his success at Uptown Records, Combs was ultimately fired by the man who gave him his first break, Andre Harrell. According to Combs, he failed to understand workplace protocols and politics, including that it took a team effort to create a record. However, his firing only increased his drive, especially to prove himself to Harrell. He applied the lessons he learned, including how to motivate people, to his next endeavor, which was wildly successful.

In 1993 he started his own record label called Bad Boy Records, and the label's first release was the Notorious B.I.G.'s debut album, *Ready to Die*. Over the next twenty years, Bad Boy Records was responsible for hip-hop and R&B talent such as Mariah Carey, Lil' Kim, and Boyz II Men. Combs was even able to hire Harrell, his former boss from Uptown Records, to work at Bad Boy Records.

When Combs was not fostering the talent of others, he was creating his own music. In 1997 he released his first single, "Can't Nobody Hold Me Down." Later that year, he released one of his most successful songs, "I'll Be Missing You," which was a tribute to his best friend, Christopher Wallace—the given name of the Notorious B.I.G.—who was murdered in March 1997. Combs's music career has earned him three Grammy Awards and countless number one hits.

Bad Boy Records is still active, with current artists including French Montana and Janelle Monáe. Christian "King" Combs, one of Combs's six children, is also signed with Bad Boy Records.

Losing Biggie

Combs was there when his best friend, Christopher "Biggie" Wallace, was murdered. In 1997 Biggie was shot through a car window while at a stoplight after leaving a large music industry party in Los Angeles, California. Combs was in the car in front of Biggie's car. Although multiple people have claimed they saw the shooter, Biggie's murder remains unsolved.

Combs has spoken about the murder in a few interviews and has expressed guilt for helping make his friend a big star, which may have led to his murder. He also explained that he and Biggie were supposed to be in London when the shooting happened. Combs had tried to convince Biggie to stick with their plans, but Biggie wanted to stay in Los Angeles that night, despite being aware that his life was in danger.

Combs says that after Biggie's death, "it was like . . . the money, the fame, the success, it didn't mean anything. It made me appreciate life, and it made me want to . . . do things for the greater good."

Quoted in Catherine Thorbecke, "Sean 'Diddy' Combs: Money, Fame and Success 'Didn't Mean Anything' After Death of Biggie Smalls," ABC News, June 23, 2017. https://abcnews.go.com.

Transforming Streetwear to Fashion

Combs had sights beyond music and expanded to fashion by starting a clothing line, Sean John, in 1998. His goal was to bring urban streetwear to the mainstream men's clothing market, and he was quickly honored for his success. In 2000 the Council of Fashion Designers of America nominated Combs as menswear designer of the year. Although he did not win that year, the nomination confirmed the merit of his fashion brand. In 2004 Combs won the award, beating designers such as Michael Kors and Ralph Lauren. His clothing, including his famous tracksuits, graced the runways and fashion magazines. One of the defining moments in his fashion career was when the Sean John flagship store opened on Fifth Avenue in New York, which he felt proved that Black designers could be a success. He later launched a girls' collection before selling the clothing company in 2016 for an estimated $70 million, according to *Forbes*.

Reflecting on his fashion legacy in 2019, Combs said, "I would say that my legacy is for all black designers. . . . Black designers have a hard time, and we're the most fashionable people on planet earth."[44] He believes that his company empowered young designers to believe in their talent.

Expanding His Business Portfolio

In addition to music and fashion, Combs has been involved in television and film as a producer and actor. He worked with MTV in *Making the Band 2* and *Making the Band 3* to discover the latest hip-hop band and all-girl group, respectively. In 2013 he launched a music-oriented television network, Revolt, which created its first digital streaming app in 2021. Before launching Revolt, he reached out to Oprah Winfrey for advice on running a network and learned that he should not overly rely on his celebrity status in building the network. In 2018 he produced a reality show on Fox called *The Four*, which was a vocal talent show intended to compete with *The Voice*.

He expanded his business portfolio even more, outside of entertainment and fashion, to include several beverage companies. For example, he partnered with actor Mark Wahlberg to create a premium water brand, AQUAhydrate. One of Combs's mentors, hedge fund manager Ray Dalio, attributes Combs's success to his ability to identify greatness. "He has a natural talent of seeing what is great—great talent in others, great products, great concepts—and intensely pursues

> "He has a natural talent of seeing what is great—great talent in others, great products, great concepts—and intensely pursues bringing them out. He also is humble and empathetic. I had no idea how humble he is until I got to know him because his public persona isn't like that."[45]
>
> —Ray Dalio, hedge fund manager

Sean Combs, well known for his hip-hop music and fashion line, controls a vast array of business ventures. The music mogul and entrepreneur continues to add to his portfolio.

bringing them out. He also is humble and empathetic. I had no idea how humble he is until I got to know him because his public persona isn't like that."[45]

Starting out, Combs believed he was providing products to customers. However, over the years, he realized that he was providing customers with a lifestyle. His diverse portfolio of business ventures—held under Combs Enterprises—was intentionally crafted to affect a person's entire day, from listening to his music in the morning, dressing in his clothes after a shower, spraying

Father's Murder

When Sean Combs was three years old, his father, Melvin Combs, was murdered. "My father . . . was a drug dealer," Combs told Revolt, his television network, in 2013. In an interview with Oprah Winfrey, Combs explained, "During [my father's] time, that was the way out of Harlem—either that or playing basketball."

Combs said that his mother lied to him about the manner of his father's death when he was little, saying, for example, that he died in a car accident. However, Combs figured out the truth when he was young.

His father's death taught him a valuable lesson: "I learned early in life there's only two ways out of that [lifestyle], dead or in jail. It made me work even harder," he says. He credits his father for inspiring him to study hard and stay off the streets. He also believes he inherited his father's "hustler spirit" and determination, which have been instrumental to his success.

Quoted in Oprah Winfrey, "Oprah Talks to Sean Combs," *O, The Oprah Magazine*, November 2006. www.oprah.com.

Quoted in Tracy, "Diddy Chokes Up Remembering His Father," Atlanta Black Star, October 24, 2013. https://atlantablackstar.com.

on his cologne before work, drinking his water at the gym, and watching his television shows at night. He has succeeded, and he credits his mother's multiple jobs for inspiring him not to overly rely on one product or business. As a result of his various business ventures, Combs is considered one of the wealthiest hip-hop artists in the world.

Despite his success, he has suffered a series of personal losses, beginning with his father as a small child; his best friend, Christopher Wallace, in his twenties; the mother to three of his children, Kim Porter, in 2018; and his friend and founder of Uptown Records, Andre Harrell, in 2020. "My family was always first, but there are countless times when I chose work over everything else," Combs said after Porter's death. "But every day I can hear her telling me to go and spend some time with the kids and make sure everybody's all right, like she would do. I'm just a lot more present, and, most important, now my kids come before anything else in my life."[46] The loss of Harrell was also devastating for Combs, who described him as a father figure for thirty years.

As younger hip-hop artists and influencers take the spotlight, Combs shows no signs of slowing down. He recently announced in an interview with *Vanity Fair* that he plans to launch an all-R&B record label because he says R&B has been abandoned. In discussing his new plans, he said he intends to create a different type of relationship between artists and the record label that resembles more of a partnership.

Supporting Education and Black Businesses

Much of Combs's philanthropy has been devoted to education. In 2003 Combs ran in the New York City Marathon to raise over $2 million to support New York City public schools, children with HIV and AIDS, and his own charity that promotes social programs. In 2016 Combs launched the Capital Preparatory Harlem Charter School, which is a free, public charter school designed for youth in Harlem. In 2021 the school announced that it would relocate to a larger facility, allowing it to serve up to seven hundred students in grades six through twelve. Combs also donated $1 million to fund a new charter school in the Bronx, which opened in 2020, and donated $1 million to fund a scholarship for business students at Howard University. Combs says, "Great schools and great education make a big difference. Unfortunately, too many people don't get the opportunity to succeed, no matter how hard they try. This is leveling the playing field."[47]

During the early part of the COVID-19 pandemic, Combs hosted a virtual dance-a-thon, which raised $3.4 million for Direct Relief, a nonprofit organization that supplies medical equipment to resource-poor communities. He also gave cash and

> "Building Black wealth starts with investing in Black-owned businesses and giving entrepreneurs access to the consumers needed to build sustainable companies that can thrive."[48]
>
> —Sean Combs

gift cards directly to families in Miami to pay rent and provide for other necessities. In addition, his company created a platform called Our Fair Share to help Black-owned businesses access the aid programs provided by the government during the pandemic. The platform was intended to raise awareness about the availability of relief funds and help Black entrepreneurs navigate the complicated application forms. It also worked to connect entrepreneurs with lenders such as banks, with whom some Black entrepreneurs do not have established relationships.

In recent interviews, Combs has been talking a lot about the importance of investing in Black-owned businesses and hinting at a new venture designed to support those businesses. On the one hundredth anniversary of the 1921 Tulsa Race Massacre, Combs announced the launch of a new venture: a digital marketplace for Black-owned brands known as Shop Circulate. When speaking of the marketplace, Combs said, "Building Black wealth starts with investing in Black-owned businesses and giving entrepreneurs access to the consumers needed to build sustainable companies that can thrive."[48] He also announced a mentorship opportunity for Black female entrepreneurs through one of his beverage companies. Although he is still actively creating his legacy, he appears to be using the business lessons he learned and his status to empower other Black entrepreneurs.

SOURCE NOTES

Introduction: Black Americans in Business

1. Quoted in Ruth Umoh and Brianne Garrett, "Black in Business: Celebrating the Legacy of Black Entrepreneurship," *Forbes*, February 3, 2020. www.forbes.com.
2. Keenan Beasley, "For Black Entrepreneurs, the Racial Wealth Gap Makes Finding Funding Nearly Impossible," *Fast Company*, July 23, 2020. www.fastcompany.com.
3. Quoted in Khristopher J. Brooks, "Why So Many Black Business Professionals Are Missing from the C-suite," CBS News, December 10, 2019. www.cbsnews.com.

Chapter One
Madam C.J. Walker: Creator of a Beauty Empire

4. Quoted in Andrew R. Chow, "Octavia Spencer to Star in 'Madam C.J. Walker' on Netflix," *New York Times*, July 30, 2018. www.nytimes.com.
5. Quoted in Henry Louis Gates Jr., "Madame Walker, the First Black American Woman to Be a Self-Made Millionaire," PBS, 2013. www.pbs.org.
6. Quoted in Sara Kettler, "How Madam C.J. Walker Invented Her Hair Care Products," Biography, January 19, 2021. www.biography.com.
7. Quoted in Emma Dibdin, "Madam C.J. Walker's Life Got the Netflix Treatment with *Self-Made*. Here's the True Story," *Town & Country*, March 20, 2020. www.townandcountrymag.com.
8. Quoted in Alice George, "How Business Executive Madam C. J. Walker Became a Powerful Influencer of the Early 20th Century," *Smithsonian*, March 21, 2019. www.smithsonianmag.com.
9. Quoted in A'Lelia Bundles, "Madam C.J. Walker Upward Bound: Hard Work and Uncanny Business Acumen Made Madam C.J. Walker a Household Name in Black America," *Baltimore (MD) Sun*, February 8, 1998. www.baltimoresun.com.
10. *New York Times*, "Walker Obituary," May 26, 1919. www.nytimes.com.

11. Quoted in BBC, "Madam CJ Walker: 'An Inspiration to Us All,'" April 5, 2020. www.bbc.com.
12. Quoted in Isis Madrid, "America's First Female Self-Made Millionaire Founded a Black Beauty Empire," *Vice*, February 16, 2018. www.vice.com.

Chapter Two
Ottawa W. Gurley: Founder of Black Wall Street

13. Quoted in White House, "Remarks by President Biden Commemorating the 100th Anniversary of the Tulsa Race Massacre," June 1, 2021. www.whitehouse.gov.
14. Quoted in Antoine Gara, "The Baron of Black Wall Street," *Forbes*, June 18, 2020. www.forbes.com.
15. Quoted in Black Wall Street USA, "Ottawa W. Gurley: The Visionary of a Generation," 2021. http://blackwallstreet.org.
16. Quoted in Ellen McGirt et al., "100 Years After the Tulsa Massacre, Black Wall Street's Legacy of Entrepreneurship Continues," *Fortune*, May 27, 2021. https://fortune.com.
17. Quoted in Alfred L. Brophy, "The Tulsa Race Riot of 1921 in the Oklahoma Supreme Court," *Oklahoma Law Review* 54, no. 1, 2001, p. 90.
18. Scott Ellsworth, "Tulsa Race Massacre," Oklahoma Historical Society. www.okhistory.org.
19. Quoted in Brooke Henderson, "Meet the Entrepreneur Who Created the First 'Black Wall Street,'" *Inc.*, December 1, 2020. www.inc.com.
20. Quoted in Gara, "The Baron of Black Wall Street."

Chapter Three
Oprah Winfrey: Media Mogul

21. Quoted in Zack Linly, "Oprah Winfrey Surprised Ron Clark Academy Educators with a Guest Appearance in Their Online Conference Call," The Root, April 25, 2020. www.theroot.com.
22. Quoted in Erin Jensen, "'The Me You Can't See': Oprah Talks About Being Molested as a Child, Breaks Down in Tears," *USA Today*, May 20, 2021. www.usatoday.com.
23. Quoted in Oprah.com, "The Teachers Who Changed Oprah's Life," February 1, 1989. www.oprah.com.
24. Oprah Winfrey, "What Oprah Knows for Sure About Finding Strength After Betrayal," Oprah.com. www.oprah.com.

25. Quoted in Sarah Berger, "Oprah Winfrey: This Is the Moment My 'Job Ended' and My 'Calling Began,'" CNBC, April 1, 2019. www.cnbc.com.
26. Quoted in ABC News, *Oprah on Oprah*, YouTube, December 10, 2010. www.youtube.com/watch?v=5hUV3Z0hU_U.
27. Quoted in Jill Disis, "The Oprah Effect: The Many Careers She Helped Launch," CNN, January 15, 2018. https://money.cnn.com.
28. Quoted in Jonathan Van Meter, "Oprah Winfrey Is on a Roll (Again)," *Vogue*, August 15, 2017. www.vogue.com.
29. Quoted in Oprah.com, "The Teachers Who Changed Oprah's Life."
30. Quoted in Hilary Weaver, "Oprah Winfrey Had Trouble Adjusting to Life After Her Talk Show," *Vanity Fair*, April 13, 2017. www.vanityfair.com.
31. Quoted in Breeanna Hare, "Winfrey Announces End of 'Oprah,'" CNN, November 20, 2009. http://edition.cnn.com.

Chapter Four
Ursula Burns: CEO of a Fortune 500 Company

32. Quoted in Lean In, "Ursula M. Burns," 2021. https://leanin.org.
33. Quoted in Alex Katsomitros, "Against the Odds: Ursula Burns' Extraordinary Rise to the Top," World Finance, April 1, 2019. www.worldfinance.com.
34. Ursula Burns, "The Worst of Times, The Best of Times," Xerox, May 22, 2009. www.news.xerox.com.
35. Quoted in NPR, "Xerox CEO: 'If You Don't Transform, You're Stuck,'" NPR, May 23, 2012. www.npr.org.
36. Quoted in Adam Bryant, "Xerox's New Chief Tries to Redefine Its Culture," *New York Times*, February 20, 2010. www.nytimes.com.
37. Quoted in Nick Wolny, "The 3 Pieces of Advice Ursula Burns' Mother Gave Her That Helped Her Become a Fortune 500 CEO," *Entrepreneur*, May 24, 2021. www.entrepreneur.com.
38. Quoted in *Fast Company*, "Fresh Copy: How Ursula Burns Reinvented Xerox," November 19, 2011. www.fastcompany.com.
39. Ursula M. Burns, *Where You Are Is Not Who You Are*. New York: Amistad, 2021.
40. Quoted in Taylor Dunn, "Former Xerox CEO Ursula Burns on Importance of STEM and Joining Uber's Board," ABC News, October 25, 2017. https://abcnews.go.com.
41. Quoted in Katsomitros, "Against the Odds."

Chapter Five
Sean Combs: Hip-Hop Mogul and Entrepreneur

42. Quoted in Andrew Barker, "Sean Combs Slams Industry's Lack of Investment in Black Enterprise, Previews Next Moves," *Variety*, July 10, 2018. https://variety.com.
43. Quoted in Roberto A. Ferdman, "Music Made Sean 'Diddy' Combs Famous, but Here's What Made Him Rich," *Washington Post*, October 2, 2015. www.washingtonpost.com.
44. Quoted in Janelle Okwodu, "Diddy at 50: The Hip-Hop Legend on His Groundbreaking Fashion Career," *Vogue*, November 4, 2019. www.vogue.com.
45. Quoted in Tressie McMillan Cottom, "'I Got a Second Chance': From Puff Daddy to Diddy to Love," *Vanity Fair*, August 3, 2021. www.vanityfair.com.
46. Quoted in Lisa Respers France, "Sean 'Diddy' Combs Reveals Kim Porter's Last Words to Him," CNN, April 24, 2019. https://edition.cnn.com.
47. Quoted in Jason Russell, "Diddy's Charter School Opens Its Doors," *Washington Examiner*, August 30, 2016. www.washingtonexaminer.com.
48. Quoted in Hilary Lewis, "Sean Combs Teams with Salesforce to Launch Digital Marketplace for Black-Owned Businesses," *Hollywood Reporter*, June 1, 2021. www.hollywoodreporter.com.

FOR FURTHER RESEARCH

Books
A'Lelia Bundles, *Self-Made*. New York: Scribner, 2020.

Ursula M. Burns, *Where You Are Is Not Who You Are*. New York: Amistad, 2021.

Chad Sanders, *Black Magic: What Black Leaders Learned from Trauma and Triumph*. New York: Simon & Schuster, 2021.

Shomari Wills, *Black Fortunes*. New York: Amistad, 2018.

Internet Sources
Jasmine Browley, "Here's Everyone on the Black Billionaire List Now," *Essence*, August 5, 2021. www.essence.com.

Catherine Clifford, "From Paper Boy to Music Mogul: Entrepreneurship Lessons from Sean 'Diddy' Combs," *Entrepreneur*, November 4, 2016. www.entrepreneur.com.

Lean In, "The State of Black Women in Corporate America," 2020. https://leanin.org.

New York Times, "What the Tulsa Race Massacre Destroyed," May 24, 2021.www.nytimes.com.

Oklahoma Commission to Study the Tulsa Race Riot of 1921, "Tulsa Race Riot: A Report by the Oklahoma Commission to Study the Tulsa Race Riot of 1921," Oklahoma Historical Society, February 28, 2001. www.okhistory.org.

Websites
A'Lelia Bundles Blog
https://aleliabundles.com/blog
As Madam C.J. Walker's biographer, A'Lelia Bundles maintains a blog with a variety of articles about her famous relative.

Black Enterprise
www.blackenterprise.com
Black Enterprise is a business, investing, and wealth-building resource for Black Americans. Although it publishes a print

magazine under the same name, Black Enterprise also maintains a website with articles, videos, and podcasts.

Minority Business Development Agency (MBDA)
www.mbda.gov
The MBDA is an agency of the US Department of Commerce that aims to assist minority-owned businesses across the country by providing grants and loans for minority-owned firms. It also provides research on minority-owned businesses.

National Museum of African American History and Culture
https://nmaahc.si.edu
The museum opened in Washington, DC, in 2016 as the nineteenth museum of the Smithsonian Institution. In addition to the physical museum, there are online resources about important Black Americans throughout history, including business leaders and entrepreneurs.

Oprah.com
www.oprah.com
Oprah Winfrey's website has information about Winfrey and her media ventures. There is a press room with news releases and photos as well as many videos from the OWN cable channel.

INDEX

Note: Boldface page numbers indicate illustrations.

Abrams, Eugene, 28
Adele, 27
Allaire, Paul, 41
AM Chicago (television talk show), 31
American Express, **6**, 7
Angelou, Maya, 35
AQUAhydrate, 50

Bad Boy Records, 48
bank loans, obtaining, 5–6
Baradaran, Mehrsa, 5
Beasley, Keenan, 7
Bell, Susie, 22
Biden, Joe, 17
billionaires in US
    first Black and first White, 5
    first Black female, 27
    number of Black, 4
Black Wall Street
    Black women and, 22
    commemorative mural, **21**
    destruction of, 17, 17
    education in, 22
    founders of, 17, 19
    growth of, 20
    origin of early residents, 19
    renamed Negro Wall Street, 20
    wealth of, 21
    worth of businesses, 26
Black Wall Street (Johnson), 20
Black women
    of Black Wall Street, 22
    empowerment of
        by Walker, 13, 15
        by Winfrey, 34, 35–36
        WomanMakers Initiative, 44–45
        Women of Black Wall Street, 22
    See also Walker, Madam C.J.; Winfrey, Oprah
Blige, Mary J., 48
Bloomberg News, 5
Board Diversity Action Alliance, 45
Branch Normal College, 18
Breedlove, Sarah. *See* Walker, Madam C.J.
Brophy, Alfred L., 23
Bundles, A'Lelia (great-great-granddaughter of Walker), 10, 11
Burns, Ursula, **40**
    early life, 37–38
    leadership positions after Xerox, 44
    in London with family, 43
    mentors, 39, 42
    Obama and, 44
    philanthropy, 44–45
    at Xerox, 37, 38, 39–44
business, obstacles, 5–7

"Can't Nobody Hold Me Down" (Combs), 48
capital, access to, 5–7
Capital Preparatory Harlem Charter School, 53
Carter, Michael, Sr., 21, 26
Chenault, Kenneth, **6**, 7
Cherokee Outlet Land Rush (Indian Territory), 18
chief executive officers (CEOs) of Fortune 500 companies
    Burns as, of Xerox, 37, 42–44
    first women, 39, 42
    number of Black, 4
    number of Black women, 45
Church, Robert Reed, 5
Color of Money, The: Black Banks and the Racial Wealth Gap (Baradaran), 5
Columbia University, 38
Combs, Christian "King," 48
Combs, Melvin, 52
Combs, Sean, **51**
    as businessperson
        beverage industry, 50
        fashion industry, 49–50
        as providing lifestyle, 51–52
        recording artist, 46
        record labels, 48, 53
        as teenager, 47
        television and film industries, 50
    careers helped by, 48
    early life, 46–47, 52
    education and, 47, 53
    importance of family, 52–53
    mentors
        Dalio, 50–51
        Harrell, Andre, 48, 52, 53
    names used by, 46, 47
    philanthropy, 53–54
    as recording artist, 48
Combs Enterprises, 51–52
Constitution, amendments, 4
Council of Fashion Designers of America, 49
COVID-19
    creation of new businesses and, 5
    medical equipment for resource-poor communities, 53

relief to individual families, 53–54
Winfrey program about, 34
COVID-19 Relief Fund, 35

Dalio, Ray, 50–51
Davis, Nancy, 13
Death in a Promised Land: The Tulsa Race Riot of 1921 (Ellsworth), 25
DeFrank-Cole, Lisa, 45
Direct Relief, 53
Dr. Phil (television talk show), 32
Duncan, Mary, 28, 32–33

Edelman, Marian Wright, 45
education
    Burns, 38
    charter schools, 53
    Combs and, 47, 53
    of Gurley, 18
    STEM, 44
    as way to empower women, 34
    Winfrey and, 28, 29, 34
Ellsworth, Scott, 25
Evans, Emma, 18, 22, 25
Events of the Tulsa Disaster (Parrish), 22

Fletcher, Viola, 24
Fortune 500 companies
    Burns, 37, 42–44
    Chenault and, 6, 7
    Mulcahy, 39, 42
    number of Black CEOs, 4
    number of Black women CEOs, 45
Four, The (television reality show), 50
Freeman, Tyrone, 16

Gates, Henry Louis, Jr., 13
Great Wonderful Hair Grower, 10
Guinness Book of World Records, 8
Gurley, Ottawa W. (Ottowa)
    death, 25
    early life, 18
    education of, 18
    as inspiration, 26
    marriage, 18
    move to Tulsa, 19–20
    real estate in Greenwood owned by, 21
    relationships with Whites, 23
    as sheriff's deputy, 23
    Tulsa Race Massacre and, 24–25
    worth of businesses owned by, before Tulsa Race Massacre, 25

Harrell, Andre, 48, 52, 53
Harry (prince of England), 29
Hicks, Wayland, 40–41
HistoryMakers, 44–45
Howard University, 47–48

I Know Why the Caged Bird Sings (Angelou), 35

"I'll Be Missing You" (Combs), 48

Jet (magazine), 47
Jim Crow laws
    business opportunities made possible by, 4–5
    described, 4, 10
    in Oklahoma, 20
Jodeci, 48
Johnson, Hannibal B., 20
Jordan, Vernon, 39

Kelly, Alice, 15
King, Gayle, 31

Lee, Hattie Mae, 28
lynchings
    fear of, in Tulsa, 24
    NAACP antilynching campaign, 14
    Stradford and, 19

Madam C.J. Walker's Gospel of Giving (Freeman), 16
Madam C.J. Walker Hair Culturists Union of America, 15
Madam C.J. Walker Manufacturing Company, 13, 16
Magic City. *See* Tulsa
Makers: Women Who Make America (television documentary), 38
Making the Band 2, 50
Making the Band 3, 50
Malone, Annie, 10, 11
McGraw, Phil, 32
McKinsey & Company, 6
McWilliams, Lelia, 9
McWilliams, Moses, 9
mentors
    Burns's, 39, 42
    Combs's
        Dalio, 50–51
        Harrell, Andre, 48, 52, 53
    Walker's, 15
    Winfrey's
        Angelou, 35
        King, 31
        teachers, 28
Me You Can't See, The (television series), 29
millionaires in US, 5, 8
Morehouse College, 34
Mulcahy, Anne, 39, 42
multi-generational wealth, 26
multilevel marketing, 13, 16

National Association for the Advancement of Colored People (NAACP), antilynching campaign, 14
National Museum of African American History and Culture, 34
Negro Cosmetics Manufacturers Association, 15
New York City Marathon, 53
New York Times, 9, 16
No Way Out (Combs), 46

O, The Oprah Magazine, 33
Obama, Barack, 44
Oklahoma land rush, 18
Oprah's Angel Network, 34
Oprah Winfrey Charitable Foundation, 34
Oprah Winfrey Leadership Academy Foundation, 34
Oprah Winfrey Network (OWN), 33
Oprah Winfrey Show, The, 27, 31–32
Our Fair Share, 54
OWN: Oprah Winfrey Network, 33

Parrish, Mary E. Jones, 22
Path Made Clear: Discovering Your Life's Direction and Purpose, The (Winfrey), 31
Peebles, R. Donahue, 6
People Are Talking (television talk show), 21
Perry, Bruce D., 29
Pleasant, Mary Ellen, 5
Polytechnic Institute of New York University, 38
population, Blacks as percentage of US, 4
Porter, Kim, 52–53

Revolt, 50
Reynolds, Violet Davis, 15
Rhimes, Shonda, 36
Rockefeller, John D., 5, 15
Rogers, John W., Jr., 26

Sean John, 49–50
segregation. *See* Jim Crow laws
Self-Made (Bundles), 10
Self-Made: Inspired by the Life of Madam C.J. Walker (Netflix series), 8
Sher, Richard, 31
Shop Circulate, 54
Smith, Robert F., 5
Stradford, John the Baptist (J.B.), 19–20, 23

Tennessee State University, 29
Tulsa
  arrest of Black man for allegedly sexually assaulting White woman, 23–24
  Greenwood Avenue/District
    commemorative mural, **21**
    destruction of, 17
    education in, 22
    growth of, 20
    origin of early residents, 19
    renamed Negro Wall Street, 20
    wealth of, 21
    worth of businesses, 26
  growth of, 19–20
  oil and, 18
  racism in, 22–23
Tulsa Race Massacre, 17, 24–25

University of Arkansas at Pine Bluff, 18
Uptown Records, 48
US Census Bureau, 4

Vanity Fair, 53

Villa Lewaro, 15

Wahlberg, Mark, 50
Walker, Charles Joseph
  as business partner, 12
  divorce, 13
  marriage, 10
Walker, Lelia (A'Leila, daughter of Walker), 9, 16
Walker, Madam C.J., **12**
  antilynching campaigns and, 14
  business model, 16
  business start, 8
  creation of Wonderful Hair Grower, 10–11
  death of, 16
  divorce, 13
  early life, 9
  empowerment of Black women by, 13, 15
  estate of, 15–16
  as laundress, 9
  legacy of, 8
  male Black business leaders and, 13–14
  marriages, 9, 10, 13
  mentor, 15
  Netflix series about, 8
  sales of hair product, 11–12, 13, 14
  Walker System for hair, 12
Walker Agents, 13
Walker Salon, 14
Wallace, Christopher "Biggie," 48, 49, 52
Washington, Booker T., 13
wealth, multi-generational, 26
wealth gap, 5
Wendy Williams Show, The (television talk show), 35
What Happened to You? Conversations on Trauma, Resilience, and Healing (Perry), 29
Where You Are Is Not Who You Are (Burns), 37
Williams, Wendy, 35–36
Wilson, Woodrow, lynchings and, 14
Winfrey, Oprah
  businesses owned by, 33–34
  characteristics, 34
  early life, 27–29
  education and, 28, 29, 34
  as host of talk shows, 27, **30**, 31–33
  influence of, 32, 35–36
  media empire of, 27
  mentors
    Angelou, 35
    King, 31
    teachers, 28
  philanthropy, 34–35
  on radio as newscaster, 29, 30
  on television as newscaster, 30–31
  violence suffered by, 28, 29
  wealth of, 23
WomanMakers Initiative, 44–45
Women of Black Wall Street (WBWS), 22

Xerox, Burns at, 37, 38, 39–44

Youngblood, Michelle, 5

PICTURE CREDITS

Cover: Phil Stafford/Shutterstock.com

6: Associated Press
12: IanDagnall Computing/Alamy Stock Photo
21: joe sohm/Joe Sohm/Visions of America/UCG/ Universal Images Group/Newscom
30: MediaPunch Inc/Alamy Stock Photo
40: Reuters/Alamy Stock Photo
51: Sipa USA via Associated Press